Moral Oblivion

Moral Oblivion

Poems by

Steve Minkin

Cover design by Shay Culligan
Cover image by Stefan Perkins

ISBN: 978-1-63980-736-9

Kelsay Books
502 South 1040 East, A-119
American Fork, Utah 84003
Kelsaybooks.com

I pray for a time of cooler heads and warmer hearts

Acknowledgments

The poems "In Need of Translation" and "The New York Times on April Fool's Day" first appeared in my book, *Where People are Trees* (Kelsay Books, 2023).

Contents

Contents

Shoelaces

I keep tying and untying my shoelaces
splitting hairs over definitions
in the absence of meanings
like little dolls bundled preterm
on the hospital floor
cold like the memories of tortured pasts
genocide, holocausts
8 million then now unimaginable
to the point of forgetting
where we came from
why we are here

My Fears November 19, 2023

I fear the chaos in thought the unexamined chaos in thought
I fear the inhumanity its power to shape events
I fear the impossibility of pausing, stepping back from the static
I fear ambient projectiles blowing up dreams
I fear the extinction of the Commandment *thou shall not kill*
I fear the bombs and cruelty
the cries of child ghosts in shrouds
I fear the deniers the justifiers
I fear indifference

When I think about the body

I recoil at the thought of killing
Chopping the chick out of human life
Emptiness when dead, crumbled, flipped, flopped
The architecture of living is mind-boggling
What a joy
To be healthy for as long as we can
And worship all others
In shapes sizes ages
Different and the same as our own

Even our cancers are processes
Gone bad, Taliban-like
Bent, broken, mutated
One that kills or awakens

But this body divine
The mind
These fears
Our spirits
Sex and conception

To kill is,
To kill or harm others
Is too big
God-like-Death

If Only the Cruel Would Step Aside

The hospital bombed
who knows how many would have survived anyway
in the absence of food water and electricity
meanwhile on the other side
the stench of the bodies still waiting to be identified
broken mutilated

littered by sorrow
amid death and despair
cruelty multiplies

Boy's Life

I know about this boy
maybe 8 or 9
because I saw him on *Al Jazeera* last night
crying

he lost most of his family
and a leg
"I want to run, walk," he said
his injured brother lying next to him

I was once boy of about 8 or 9
it was a time that seemed to last forever

Standing Before God

warriors
who among you
is righteous
humane
pious
moral
repentant

who among you
will be possessed by nightmares
haunted by shame
filled with dread

who is unreclaimed
boastful
couldn't care less

White Against White

rows of bodies
wrapped in white
little corpses unnamed

the President pardons
2 white turkeys,
Liberty and *Bell*

We gather with family and friends

Our Lady of Vladimir

Baby Jesus touches your face
legend has it that Luke the Evangelist
painted the image from life
it was you who saved Moscow
from the Tatar hordes
most sacred icon of Russian identity
and Orthodox Church

Blessed Virgin
maker of miracles
won't you shed a tear
incanting your name
priests bless recruits
destined for Ukraine

IKEA

the day of the invasion
in the Blockbuster Mall
close to the heart of Kiev
more than 20 thousand individual items were for sale
along with Swedish meatballs

In Need of Translation

She gave me two books
of her poetry
a Syrian woman
years ago in Paris
she was attractive
we were drawn

married with children
excellent English
we talked for hours   stayed in adjacent rooms
at the top of our small hotel
we shared a bathroom
she was afraid of the dark
kept her door ajar

she gave me her books
covers romantically surreal
years before the birth and death of
the Arab Spring

is there a place for poetry
amid unrelenting evil
barrel bombs   gassed children
cities in ruins
a balm of rhyme and harmony
for refugees
a future in the face of slaughter

Detritus

so handsome   smile so big
Black, the police couldn't stop harassing him
19-years-old in the Marines
1967–68
moral oblivion
body bags heaped
tens of thousands
blood-soaked grotesque
the worst part of the war

he returned with
Death in his eyes

homeless
heroin
self-medicating
addicted
withdrawal
bad papers
no benefits
no treatment
War on Drugs

imprisoned veterans
tens of thousands
languishing decades

Ho Chi Minh's Garden

In my convalescence
music
carried me to the colonial center of Hanoi
to the grove
where Ho Chi Min
lived
near the lake where John McCain
fell from the sky

the grove was a place
where poets
contemplated the heavens
bombs
monsoon rain

petals falling from trees
flowers in phosphorus light
napalmed blossoms
passing memories
as the meds kick in

Path-ology

you stayed on the path
farmed your fields
married at the right time
prayed
harvested grapes
attended to the olive trees
sent your daughter to school
herding goats she
dreamed of becoming an engineer

politicians, generals, bureaucrats,
knowing nothing of olive trees
the abundance of grapes
or goat herders studying trigonometry
far away men make serious plans
their construction of events
destroys everything

past obliterated
crossing borders
refugee-fodder for demagogues

Lieutenant D. Tortured Leila Djabali in Algeria

She wrote "Pour mon tortionnaire, le Lieutenant D." ("For My Torturer, Lieutenant D.," 1957) while imprisoned at Barberousse Prison in Algiers.

her face bleeding
"You slapped me
no one had ever slapped me"
and electric shocks
abuse hands all over and in her body
and decades later
I am moved because
she wrote a poem
addressed to her tormenter
Lieutenant D.
as he looked in the mirror
carefully combing his hair

MbS

the Crown Prince and his closest friends
hosted the New York Times columnist
a late-night feast
lambs freshly slaughtered
succulent
the reporter licking his fingers
praises the energetic the Saudi ruler
"a modernizer" he wrote
while hours away
hundreds of thousands
starving in Yemen
a princely famine
billions spent on fighter aircraft
and bombs sold by the USA
paid for in cash

Gulf & Golf

scores
beheaded
young and old
for words
wishes
religious beliefs

the Arabian sword
sliced his neck
the teenager
who rashly posted the word *Democracy*

think of him every time
a player slices a ball
now that the Saudis
are heavily invested
in golf

19 Children and One Teacher Murdered

Seeing you, I cannot fathom the mystery—
how did you become mine?
—Rabindranath Tagore, "Birth Talk" (trans. Sajed Kamal)

you looked so happy this morning
so handsome my pride and joy
only yesterday I wiped away a tear
only this morning I combed your hair
after breakfast kissed your forehead,
letting you go to the safety of school
primary school
your smiling teachers
morning circle a meditation on possibilities
the unfolding of a happy Tuesday
tasks for the day—handing out snacks
feeding the goldfish

Majestic Innocence

I stumbled upon
a bald eagle
up close
in a nearby New Hampshire wood
a species nearly extinct
eggshells so soft they collapsed
the woe of DDT

saved by Rachel Carson
and environmental regulations
the fate of bald eagles and their raptor cousins
rests in the hands of Supreme Court,
philosophical originalists
who see nothing in the Constitution
regarding the rights of birds

Cassandra's Pot (2024)

"God should be dead,"
one lobster told the other inside the trap
"I thought we'd be in the sea forever," said the other
even as the prophets foretold
of boiling water, cracked shells and butter

Globally 2024 was the hottest year on record

Shameful

in front of our very eyes
time is being dragged backward in Florida
one hundred and sixty years after the Emancipation Proclamation
children are now legally required to learn
about the benefits of slavery
slave master myths
used to justify whips, torture, rape
the buying and selling of humanity

Critical Race History

a compromise
toiling
three-fifths
pulling stumps out of swamp-ovens
filled with poisonous snakes
making levees
for cotton plantations
wealth builders
for the decedents of Scots
fleeing the brutality of the English

wealth builders
bound
whipped
toiling
tortured
kidnapped
raped
sold
blazing sun
freezing cold
mothers and daughters
boys and men
their value being
bales of cotton

chain ganged
race-riot-disposed
segregated
redlined

lynchings
now captured on cell phones

Black bodies swinging in the Southern Breeze
Strange fruit hanging from the Poplar trees

Last lines from "Strange Fruit," a poem by Abel Meeropol, recorded by Billie Holliday in 1939.

The New York Times on April Fool's Day

I ran out of coffee filters

Oh my god
It's raining out and I am suffering from a rare hangover
not a big hangover but a bottle of wine left
at my exhausted apartment
was red-filled-thick, blood-like, old-blood

I needed a transfusion, something different
as night moved to morning hours, I consumed the bottle of wine

On the radio—Radio Free Brattleboro
Michael asks his guest, *What do you do when your
    spiritual,religious tradition doesn't do it for you?*

I walked down the street
for the comfort of coffee and the morning paper
my fix with the New York Times

The April Fools Edition
stomach-turning photos
of dismembered employees of a security firm
hanging on a bridge over the Euphrates River
hanging charred among the joyous descendants of the start of
    civilization
the descendants of Noah, Adam and Eve

The spiritual healer on the radio
talks about enjoying the richness of one's own traditions
"We don't know where we are going but we have to get there."

My coffee, "Hometown Brew"
The pot was empty
I had to wait

I returned to reading
about Fallujah and the deep hatred of Americans
there

On the radio, her voice transcendent, the guest asks, "What is
    worse than Death?"

"Birth."

April 1, 2004

A Student Explained

"I would rather die serving my country than die at 19 injecting
   drugs."
He expects to be able to retire from the Marines at 36 and is not
   afraid of death.

Haiku:

overdose at 19
retire from Marines at 36
or die for country

Jawbone

you who sins against the Marines
has earned
so you say "political capital"
and plan to spend it

like so many smashed
jaw bones
and testicles

blood tissue
and organs

at the exchange rate of say,
100 Marines equals1,500
Iraqis

a friendly white face
lips dripping with
blood
Marine blood, Iraqi blood
a red painted mask
national security
necrotic cannibal
tribe of feasting
thieves

choosing death to life
war to peace
mutilated
Iraqis and Marines

if there be heaven and hell
may you spend eternity in Falluja
a nightmare of blown apart faces
haunted capital
jaw bones, tissue, organs
big necks and absent arms
gaping spurting wounds

Deep Space

In a parallel universe
on a habitable planet
Russians and Ukrainians
fly missiles
back and forth
every day
colorful missiles
filled with gifts for children

why not,
when love and compassion are commonplace, they multiply *ad
    infinitum*

hands reach out
arms so long
help is always there
mana falls from heaven
people innocently love
no one goes hungry

when astrophysicists
find and study our twin
they may discover
why on Earth
children fail to change the world

Soap

One two three four five
oh yes
digits of one hand
the members of my family
mother, father, brother, brother
and for many years
bicycles, squirrels and God
oh yes—I had what you would call
a personal relationship
often on the way to synagogue
I can't remember what we talked about
mostly I walked alone to *shul*
I remember the Korean War
there was a photo
I'd seen of a dead soldier
clean cut—a crew cut
he was lying face down
seeing where the bullet
entered the back of his head
he seemed young even to me at seven
I remember atom bomb drills
we would go out to the hall to get our coats
and then go under our desks
coats over our heads
I felt secure
protected by my coat and desk
whereas at night in bed
I worried about the bomb
I remember images on TV
mounds of bodies
piles of Jews
and people their bones showing

starved
haunted Jews in striped jackets
I remember talking to God
about this
I often talked to God
and in Sunday school
I'd bring 15 cents to buy a stamp
for a tree in Israel
knowing that the Jews there
were making the desert bloom
and that there was a tree there with my name
I remember the terror of my Bar Mitzvah service
not being well prepared but how I knew the
Saturday service by heart
I remember we had poor seats in the back
during the High Holidays
and walking with Michael Adlerstein,
who became a physicist, talking about God
I remember the rabbi I loved—a man of the mind-
his sermons my introduction to the intellect
and the disappointment I felt when I was in college
because he failed to condemn Vietnam,
that Jews should side with civil rights and oppose
the war,
this put an end to my conversations with God
I remember, as a child, spinning the globe
my finger landing on different countries
and how I knew one day I would move faraway
I remember being told many times
"You don't look Jewish"

About the Author

Steve Minkin collects whispers and shouts. He writes poetry and prose in Southern Vermont.

www.ingramcontent.com/pod-product-compliance
Lightning Source LLC
Chambersburg PA
CBHW051434090426
42737CB00014B/2972